Otto Goldschmidt

Jenny Lind

A record and analysis

Otto Goldschmidt

Jenny Lind
A record and analysis

ISBN/EAN: 9783337140724

Printed in Europe, USA, Canada, Australia, Japan

Cover: Foto ©Andreas Hilbeck / pixelio.de

More available books at **www.hansebooks.com**

Jenny Lind

JENNY LIND

A RECORD AND ANALYSIS OF THE "METHOD"

OF THE LATE

MADAME JENNY LIND-GOLDSCHMIDT

By W. S. ROCKSTRO

TOGETHER WITH A SELECTION OF

CADENZE, SOLFEGGI, ABELLIMENTI, &c.

IN

ILLUSTRATION OF HER VOCAL ART

EDITED BY

OTTO GOLDSCHMIDT.

PRICE TWO SHILLINGS.

LONDON & NEW YORK

NOVELLO, EWER AND CO.

—

1894.

All those portions of the following pages which have already been published are here reprinted from the work entitled

JENNY LIND THE ARTIST

(London, 1891 : John Murray),

by kind permission of Mr. Murray.

The Portrait is from an engraving by William Holl, after a daguerreotype by Kilburn, London, 1848.

TO

SIGNOR MANUEL GARCIA

(Knight of the Order of Gustavus Vasa; M.D., Königsberg; etc., etc.)

THE FOLLOWING PAGES ARE DEDICATED

AS A TRIBUTE OF SINCERE ADMIRATION

BY

OTTO GOLDSCHMIDT

AND

W. S. ROCKSTRO.

THE VOCAL METHOD

OF

MADAME JENNY LIND-GOLDSCHMIDT.

THOSE who had the good fortune to hear Mdlle. Jenny Lind sing, either on the Stage or in the Concert-room, after her artistic ideal had been fully matured, and while her voice was in its fullest perfection, cannot fail to remember the beautiful *Cadenze* which lent so distinctive a charm to many of her songs, or the passages of brilliant *fioritura* with which some of her masterpieces of Italian vocalisation were embellished.

The originality of these *Cadenze*, and other embellishments, was so striking, and their charm so potent, that, in the year 1891, the authors of the Memoir, entitled JENNY LIND THE ARTIST, thought it desirable to include a few of them in the " Musical Appendix " with which that work was supplemented, with the view of ensuring their preservation to posterity ; and it is believed that this end will be still farther secured by their publication, with the addition of a few more examples, in a separate form. It is in the hope of attaining this object that the following pages are presented to the public, in full assurance that the rising generation of vocalists cannot fail to be profited by the study of *Solfeggi*, and other like passages, bequeathed to the world by one of the greatest singers of the present century.

In order that this desirable result may be the more certainly obtained, it is necessary that the *Cadenze* in question should be prefaced by a clear and categorical account of certain circumstances connected with the *timbre* and compass of Mdlle. Lind's voice, and some of the more important characteristics of her method of voice-production ; including some points which, before the publication of the work above alluded to, were known only to a few of her intimate friends.

Mdlle. Lind's artistic career began at a very early age ; but, unhappily, she had no opportunity of studying under an experienced Maëstro of the highest order until she had nearly completed her twenty-first year. Her voice at that period had suffered much, both from over-exertion and the want of that

careful management which can only be acquired by long and
diligent training under a thoroughly competent teacher.   She
had tried to reach her high ideal by the only means she knew of—
means very pernicious indeed.   The result was, that the voice
had been cruelly injured, the mischief being, moreover, seriously
aggravated by the fatigue consequent upon a long and harassing
provincial tour, undertaken in her native Sweden, in the spring
of the year 1841, for the purpose of acquiring the means necessary
to secure for her a long and indispensable term of rest from
theatrical engagements and an opportunity for diligent private
study.

Alarmed at the chronic hoarseness and other marked
symptoms of deterioration from which the vocal organs were
suffering at this period, she determined to seek a competent
teacher in Paris; where, towards the close of August, 1841, she
was received as a pupil by Signor Manuel Garcia, the most
talented and successful master then living.

Under this unrivalled *Maëstro di Canto* she studied diligently,
from the last week in August, 1841, until the summer of 1842;
by which time she had learned all that it was possible for any
master to teach her. `

The result for which she had so perseveringly laboured was
now attained.   Her voice, no longer suffering from the effect of
the cruel fatigue, and the inordinate amount of over-exertion
which had so lately endangered, not merely its well-being, but
its very existence, had by this time far more than recovered its
pristine vigour—it had acquired a rich depth of tone, a sympathetic *timbre*, a birdlike charm in the silvery clearness of its
upper register, which at once impressed the listener with the
feeling that he had never before heard anything in the least
degree resembling it.   No human organ is perfect.   It is quite
possible that other voices may have possessed qualities which
this did not ; for, voices of exceptional beauty are nearly always
characterised by an individuality of *timbre* or expression which
forms by no means the least potent of their attractions.   The
natural flexibility of the Contessa de' Rossi's* voice was pheno-
menal.   Mdlle. Alboni's involuntary *vibrato* breathed a languid
tenderness of passion which could never have been attained
by any amount of study.   But the listener never stopped

---

* Mdlle. Sontag, afterwards Contessa de' Rossi.

to analyse the qualities of Mdlle. Lind's voice, the marked individuality of which set analysis at defiance. By turns full, sympathetic, tender, sad, or brilliant, it adapted itself so perfectly to the artistic conception of the song it was interpreting, that singer, voice, and song were one. Time had been when, from sheer lack of technical knowledge, she had been unable to give expression to her high ideal ; when her method was as yet too unformed for the utterance of her grand conception of the parts of *Agatha* and *Euryanthe*, of *Pamina* and *Donna Anna*, of *La Vestale* and *Alice*, and *Amina*, and *Norma*, and *Lucia ;* all of which she had already sung, in Stockholm, and felt deeply, and made her hearers feel, by resistless force of sympathy alone, though every one had fallen short of the perfect artistic interpretation which can only be attained when the poetry of the mental conception is supported by an amount of technical skill equal to its demands. But this time had passed away, for ever. Her voice was now so completely under command, that its obedience to every changing phase of the singer's thoughts, to every demand of the composer's genius, was absolute and instantaneous. All the technical perfection that could be attained by unlimited perseverance, under the guidance of an enlightened teacher, she had gained since her arrival in Paris; the rest she had always possessed, for it was part of herself. She was born an artist ; and, under Garcia's guidance, had now become a *virtuosa.* The scales, sung " slowly up and down, with great care," and the " awfully slow shake,"* practised under his direction, had borne abundant fruit. Followed by exercises of a more advanced character, they had resulted in producing a facility of execution which serves materially to strengthen our faith in the legendary stories told of Farinelli and " Il Porporino," Signore Strada, and Cuzzoni, and Faustina, the Cavaliere Nicolini, and other marvellous vocalists of the eighteenth century, whose feats of skill have been described by admiring contemporaries in such terms of rapture, that one class of modern critics has been tempted to reject the whole story as a gross exaggeration, while another school would have us believe that the art of vocalisation, as practised in that golden age, is lost beyond all

---

* So described by Mdlle. Lind in a letter, written at the time, to a friend in Sweden.

possibility of recovery. There is no logical necessity for the
acceptance of either of these trenchant theories. The music
written for, and sung by, those giants of a bygone age, proves
that the stories told of their marvellous power are in nowise
exaggerated. Handel wrote passages, in *Riccardo Primo*, which
no singer now living could execute ; and equally trying divisions,
in *Ariadne, Rinaldo*, and other Operas, for the Cavaliere
Nicolini, Carestini, Signora Strada, and Senesino. The Operas
of Porpora and Hasse abound with similar passages for
Farinelli, and " Il Porporino," Faustina, and their great contemporaries of the Italian School. No one now attempts to
grapple with these monstrous *tours de force ;* but Mdlle. Lind
proved them to be still attainable by exceptional talent, supplemented by equally exceptional perseverance. The assumption
that the art has been lost is absurd. The method may have
been neglected, and temporarily forgotten. We do not deny
that. But there is not—or ought not to be—the possibility of
such a thing as a "lost art." What has been done once can be
done again. And it would be difficult, in the face of the *Cadenze*
here given to the public, to imagine any *tour de force*—whether
involving difficulty of intonation, or rapidity of execution,
prolonged sustaining - power, or contrasts obtainable by
apparently unlimited exercise of the *messa di voce*—of which
Mdlle. Lind was incapable, after the completion of her course of
study. One great secret—perhaps the greatest of all—the key
to the whole mystery connected with this perfect mastery over
the technical difficulties of vocalisation—lay in the fortunate
circumstance that Signor Garcia was so " very particular
about the breathing."* For the skilful management of the
breath is everything ; and she learned to fill the lungs with such
dexterity that, except with her consent, it was impossible to
detect either the moment at which the breath was renewed, or
the method by which the action was accomplished. We say,
" except with her consent," because, on the stage, there are
moments when, for dramatic effect, the act of breathing has
itself a rhetorical, or, in extreme cases, even a passionate
significance ; when the correct delivery of the words demands
that breath should be taken, without any attempt at disguise,
in accordance with the grammatical punctuation of the text ;

---

* Extract from the letter mentioned in the previous foot-note.

and of this means of expression she fully appreciated the value. But where pure vocalisation was concerned, and unbroken continuity became an imperious artistic necessity, the moment at which the lungs were replenished remained as profound a secret as it did in the performances of Rubini—who, fortunately for him, possessed a much greater natural capacity for abundant inspiration, and had therefore a less amount of difficulty to overcome in bringing his art to the ineffable perfection he so well succeeded in attaining. The result was the same in both cases; but, in the one, it was materially aided by a happy physical organisation, while, in the other, it was wholly the effect of art—an art which, though possible to all, is so difficult to acquire that, through want, in most cases, of the necessary perseverance, not one singer out of a hundred succeeds in attaining it, even in a moderate degree.

Signor Frederic Lablache once told a friend of the writer that, when singing, on one occasion, with Rubini, in the *Matrimonio Segreto*, he held the great Tenor's hand in his own, during a passage in the famous duet, and, at the same time, looked him full in the face, without being able to detect the act of breathing in the least degree. This wonderful power of concealment led to the belief that Rubini could sing during the act of inspiration! Of course, it was simply the triumph of consummate art, misunderstood only by those who were ignorant of the first principles of singing. An absurd story was even invented, to the effect that he, who never forced a note, and whose vocal registers were more perfectly equalised, more delicately blended into one than those of any other tenor that ever existed, once broke his collar-bone in the attempt to deliver a mighty *Si de poitrine* by aid of a violent effort of clavicular breathing! He was just as likely to have broken his neck and fallen dead on the spot. Yet, to this day, the story is cited as an instance of the dangers of a vicious method of filling the lungs: a proof that the study of breathing is still recognised as a necessary part of the singer's education, though the tale could never have obtained credence, had not the method pursued by the two great artists of whom we are speaking been hopelessly misunderstood.

With the rare powers at her command, Mdlle. Lind was able, without effort, to give expression to every phase of the artistic conception which she had formed by the exercise of innate genius. Her acting had grown up with her from her infancy, and formed part of her inmost being. She had, indeed, gained experience by observation of others, and, calmly passing judgment upon her own performance, had carefully thought out the matter; and the result was that the acting and the singing had become so closely interwoven with each other, that they naturally united in the formation of one single conception. Each part as she interpreted it to herself was a consistent whole, dramatic and musical, breathing poetry and romance from beginning to end; yet, as true to nature as she was herself, and no longer fettered by the fatal technical weakness which had so long stood between the ideal and its perfect realisation.

Mdlle. Lind's voice was a brilliant and powerful Soprano, combining the volume and sonority of the true *Soprano drammatico*—to which class of voices it unquestionably belonged—with the lightness and flexibility peculiar to the more ductile and airy *Soprano sfogato*, with the characteristic tenuity of which it had, however, nothing in common.

Its compass extended from B below the stave, to G on the fourth line above it—in technical language, from b to $\bar{\bar{g}}$; that is to say, a clear range of two octaves and three-quarters, as shown in the subjoined diagram:—

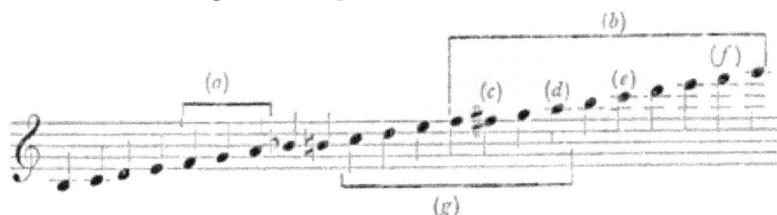

(*a*) The veiled notes in the middle register.

(*b*) The brilliant head voice.

(*c*) The F♯ which forms so striking a feature in Mendelssohn's *Elijah*.

(*d*) The ringing upper A, used with such thrilling effect in the opening movement of *Casta diva*.

(*e*) The upper C, forming, with the above-mentioned A, the initial passage in the *Tanzlied aus Dalekarlien*—a Scandinavian air, which Mdlle. Lind sang, with great effect, both in England and Germany.

(*f*) The F in alt, introduced by Mozart in *Non paventar*.

(*g*) The six natural notes (C, D, E, F, G, A) in the youthful voice, to be presently described.

The various registers of this extended compass were so skilfully blended into one, by the effect of art, that it was impossible for the most delicate or attentive ear to detect their points of junction. In fact, after the completion of its cultivation under the guidance of Signor Garcia, the entire voice became one homogeneous whole, so even in its calibre, that the notes were avowedly sung without a thought as to the best way of "placing" them.

Certain regions, however, possessed marked æsthetic qualities, very clearly distinguishable, though they could be modified, at will, in accordance with the demands of the passages into which they were introduced. For instance, three notes of the middle register (the F, G, and A, shown at (a) in the diagram) were invested, in *piano* passages, with a veiled tone of ravishing beauty—as in the long-drawn A, in the middle register, which forms the opening note of *Casta diva*. These three notes were more seriously injured than any other region of the voice, by the hard work and faulty method of production that had been forced upon Mdlle. Lind before her journey to Paris. It is well known to every experienced *Maēstro di Canto*, that more voices are injured by the attempt to sing these three important notes in the lower instead of in the middle register, than by any other error of production whatever; and there can be no doubt that it was this error that caused so much trouble to Mdlle. Lind, who, notwithstanding the beautiful tone by which the notes in question were afterwards characterised, assured Fröken Signe Hebbe* that she believed that they "never became quite right."

The F♯ was so much admired by Mendelssohn, that he constantly used it in *Hear ye, Israel*, and other parts of *Elijah*. The A above it, was brought prominently forward in a syncopated passage in the slow movement of *Casta diva;* and the same A, with the C above it, formed the first two notes in one of Mdlle. Lind's famous Swedish Melodies.

It was remarkable that these exceptionally high notes, though brilliant beyond description, when used at their full power, could be reduced to a *pianissimo* as perfect as that of the veiled tones of the middle register. The *pianissimo*, indeed, was one of

---

* A dramatic singer at Stockholm, who lately published an account of her intercourse with Madame Goldschmidt, in a Swedish newspaper.

the most beautiful features of Mdlle. Lind's singing.   It reached
to the remotest corner of the largest theatre or concert-room in
which she sang ; it was as rich and full as her *mezzo-forte ;* yet
it was so truly *piano* that it fell upon the ear with the charm of
a whisper, only just strong enough to be audible.   The reader
will be interested in hearing that Her Majesty regarded this
pianissimo as one of the most beautiful characteristics of
Mdlle. Lind's singing, and Chopin spoke of its "charm" as
" indescribable."

A wholly different effect—though bearing a certain sort of
analogy to this—was produced in the *Norwegian Echo Song*
by a peculiar tightening of the throat, which Madame Goldschmidt once tried to explain to the writer, though the process
was so purely subjective that she said it was almost impossible
to describe it in words.   The effect produced so nearly resembled
that of a natural echo, reverberated from the opposite wall, that
it never failed to mystify an audience before which it was
presented for the first time.

The notes, C, D, E, F, G, A, marked (*g*) in our diagram,
were noticed by Mdlle. Lind, at a very early period, as the best
notes of her voice.   And judging, from their position in the scale,
that her voice was intended by Nature to resolve itself into a
Soprano of exceptional height, she practised these notes, with
the semitones between them, more diligently than any others,
with the full determination to extend the process until the tone
of the remaining portions of the voice became as rich, as pure,
and as powerful as that of the six notes which she regarded as
forming the fundamental basis of the whole.   How fully she
succeeded in carrying out this intention we know already ; and
it is scarcely too much to say, that it was to this firm resolve,
and the clear foresight which prompted it, that her ultimate
success is mainly to be attributed.

Mdlle. Lind's voice was not by nature a flexible one.   The
rich sustained tones of the *soprano drammatico* were far more
congenial to it, than the rapid execution which usually charac-
terises the lighter class of *soprano* voices.   But this she attained
also, by almost superhuman labour.   Her perseverance was
indefatigable.   Among the *Cadenze* with which she was accus-
tomed to embellish her favourite airs was one adapted to a
movement from *Beatrice di Tenda*, introducing a scale passage
ascending chromatically to the upper E flat, and then descending

in the same manner.* She once, while at the zenith of her career, told Fröken Signe Hebbe that she had practised such passages all her life, but that it was only quite lately that she had succeeded in satisfying herself with them; adding, that she never allowed herself to indulge in singing exceptionally difficult passages before the public, until she had thoroughly mastered them, but preferred simplifying them to running the risk of an imperfect rendering of the notes.

Another remarkable feature in Mdlle. Lind's singing was the shake, which she delivered, at will, either with unapproachable brilliancy, or in the form of a whisper, more like the warbling of a bird than the utterance of a human voice.

Though it is necessary that a perfect shake should always begin with, and lay the metrical accent continuously upon, the written note, it is notorious that most shakes fail through want of attention on the part of the singer to the upper auxiliary or unwritten note. The general tendency is to let this note gradually flatten, until, in very bad cases, the distance between the two notes is diminished from a tone to little more than a semitone. So well is this fact known, that the late Mr. Cipriani Potter once told the writer how he had been taught, in his youth, to separate the notes so widely that "a cocked hat could be thrown between them." Mdlle. Lind devised a cure for this corrupt delivery of the shake. In teaching, she *began* by impressing the *upper* note upon the ear, as the most important, at this early stage of the process, both as to strength and duration; leaning, as it were, upon it, and slurring up to it from the lower interval. She employed for this purpose, first, the leap of a fifth, then that of a fourth, and so on, until she reached the tone, or semitone, continuing the shake exercise between the two intervals, *whatever their distance,* for some time, before proceeding from the wider intervals to a lesser one; always adhering to the upper note as, at this stage, the most important one; and always making beginners practise it with extreme slowness.

The following exemplification of this particular exercise, written by herself, a few years ago, for the guidance of a young vocalist, and illustrating the way in which she not only practised

the shake herself, but also, in later years, taught it to others,
has been found among her music :—

At a later period of instruction, the notes marked (*a*) and (*b*)
were to be omitted, and the succession of intervals blended into
one continuous exercise, thus :—

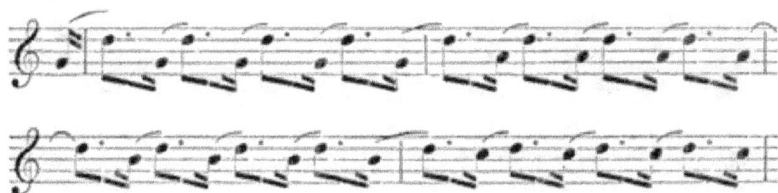

But it was not until after considerable advance had been
made, that the exercise was allowed to be sung with any degree
of quickness.

When, at last, after diligent practice, the perfect shake was
attained, it was sung with the rhythmic accent on the real or
written note, thus :—

not thus :—

The various effects we have here attempted to describe would
have been impossible, but for that skilful management of the
breath of which we had occasion to speak when treating of

Mdlle. Lind's studies under the guidance of Signor Garcia. Her chest had not the natural capacity of Mdlle. Alboni's or Signor Rubini's; but she renewed her breath so rapidly, so quietly, so cleverly, that the closest observer could never detect the moment at which the lungs were replenished; and, by the outside world, her extraordinary sustaining power was attributed to abnormal capacity of the lungs. The apparent ease with which she attained this difficult end was due to an artfully-studied combination of the processes technically termed "*costal*" and "*clavicular breathing*"; in the first of which—used only after the completion of a distinct phrase of the vocal melody—the lower part or "base" of the lungs, freed from the last remains of the previous breath, is refilled, to its utmost capacity, without undue precipitation, yet with sufficient rapidity to answer all practical purposes; while in the second—used for the continuation of phrases too long for delivery within the limits of a single inspiration—the lungs are neither completely *emptied*, nor completely *refilled*, but *replenished* only, by means of a gentle inhalation, confined to that portion of the organ which lies immediately beneath the *claviculæ*, or collar-bones. The skill with which these two widely different processes were interchanged, when circumstance demanded their alternate employment, was such as can only be acquired by long and unwearied practice, untrammelled by prejudice either for or against any special method whatever; and it is not too much to say, that it was to the sustaining power, acquired by this careful management of the breath, that Mdlle. Lind owed her beautiful *pianissimo*, and that marvellous command of the *messa di voce* which enabled her to swell out a *crescendo* to its utmost limit, and follow it, without a break, with a *diminuendo* which died away to an imperceptible point, so completely covering the end of the note that no ear could detect the moment at which it faded into silence.

Within the last few years, an attempt has been made to connect the term, *clavicular breathing*, with a mode of filling the lungs, pernicious, to the last degree—a process which, we need scarcely say, was never practised, either by Mdlle. Lind or Rubini, whose method of breathing seems to have been closely analogous to, if not absolutely identical with her own. True clavicular breathing is not only a perfectly legitimate process, but one quite indispensable to the accomplished vocalist.

It is necessary that we should speak very clearly on this point, since Mdlle. Lind's method of breathing has sometimes been quite misunderstood, and stories have been told of it, both in print and in open discussion, as absurd as those circulated with relation to Rubini. Only a few years ago, her method was publicly described, in terms so incorrect that they could only lead to the wildest misconception of the truth.

And no less complete was Mdlle. Lind's command over the difficulties of articulation than over those of vocalisation pure and simple. Her delivery of the difficult—we had almost said, impossible—passage in the grand *scena* from *Der Freischütz—Täuscht das Licht des Monds mich nicht!*[*]—though so clear and distinct that not a syllable lost its full meaning, was nevertheless so soft and smooth that it could scarcely have been surpassed in Italian. We do not hesitate to say that she was the only great singer by whom we have heard this famous *crux* surmounted without a trace of harshness in the delivery of the words. On one occasion Madame Birch-Pfeiffer left her, alone, practising the word *zersplittre* ("to shiver to pieces"), on a high B flat, in the opening Recitative in *Norma ;* and, returning several hours afterwards, found her still practising the same word. And she continued to practise it, until she succeeded in pronouncing it quite perfectly on the high note, though few even of the best German vocalists attain a better pronunciation than *zersplättre*. But she never erred in the delivery of even the most difficult word in any language whatsoever. So perfect was the mastery she exercised over larynx, throat, lips, tongue, teeth, soft palate, each and all, that never a syllable was stifled at its birth, never a vowel-sound corrupted in its passage through the longest groups of mingled leap, arpeggio, or scale. It was this high quality that lent so powerful a charm to the complicated "divisions," the rapid passages of *fioritura*, of which Lablache, in describing them to Madame Grisi, said that "every note was a pearl." The purity of the vowel-sound, by which the pearls were strung together, secured their perfect equality of tone and *timbre ;* and, whether the most rapid notes were sung *legato*, or *staccato*, they either ran on velvet, or rang out sharply and clearly as the touch of a *mandoline*. The *technique*, in either case, was absolutely faultless, and its

---

[*] " Does not the light of the moon deceive me ! "

perfection was entirely the result of hard work, indefatigable practice, unwearying study. To the end of her career, she never sang in the evening without preparing for the performance by practising for a long time, earlier in the day—always *a mezza voce*, to avoid fatiguing the voice unnecessarily, but never sparing the time or trouble. And herein lay the secret of her victory over difficulties which tempt so many less courageous aspirants to despair.

Undoubtedly, the "method" thus diligently cultivated was, in many points, subjective. We possess, however, a letter written by her to her friend, Fräulein von Jaeger, at Vienna, which enters into some particulars connected with our present subject of consideration, so curiously interesting, that we cannot refrain from presenting them *in extenso* :—

"Ems, June 8, 1855.

"And what is my good Gusti doing? Is she working as industriously as ever at her singing?

"The chief thing that I have to say, to-day, concerns that part of Friedrich Schmitt's 'Singing School' of which you wish for an explanation.*

"I do not think you have rightly understood the point. Read the paragraph again and it will surely become clearer to you.

"Naturally, he does not mean that you are to attack a note twice; but that, before you sound the note, the larynx must be properly prepared in the position in which the forthcoming sound lies, whether high or low. The result of this is a firm attack; and, as soon as you have sounded one note, you must spring so nimbly on all those above—or below it—that no rift can be detected between the sounds; and, in this way, the completion of the phrase is accomplished without a break. For instance, the notes

must so hang together that they make one whole; and this results from binding and striking them, at one and the same time—if I may so express myself—though it is almost impossible

---

* "Grosse Gesang-Schule für Deutschland," von Friedrich Schmitt (München, 1854); a work of which Madame Goldschmidt thought so highly, that she permitted her testimonial to be printed in connection with it.

to explain this clearly in words. But I have often spoken to
my Gusti about this and shown it to her. It lies in the
flexibility of the larynx, and must therefore be practised. Sing
your exercise, then, so that this flexibility of the throat may be
quickly developed. The attack of the single notes will thus be
improved; and the string of notes will follow."

Madame Goldschmidt was quite right in saying that " it
is almost impossible to explain this clearly in words." No one
knew better than she did that the best " Singing Schools " that
ever were published are useless without the aid of a teacher ;
for, until she found a teacher in Signor Garcia, she wandered
daily farther and farther from the true paths, until, in the end,
her voice but narrowly escaped from utter destruction. When
once the truth was pointed out to her, her quick perception and
unerring musical instinct enabled her to grasp it at a glance ;
and, when once she began to practise upon true principles, the
difficulties she had formerly experienced with regard to the
method of voice-production were at an end.

On one point she always insisted very strongly. She had an
innate hatred of the contortions with which so many vocalists of
inferior order disfigure their features when delivering the
passages they wish to render most impressive. She was never
satisfied with a song, unless the singer " looked pleasant."
She regarded singing as a beautiful gift of Nature ; a gift for
which those who possess it should feel truly thankful, and
proclaim their thankfulness by the expression of their features.
She had a horror of careless articulation, even in speaking.
And she felt firmly persuaded that the practice of singing, on
the true " method," tended to the invigoration of the body, and
especially of a weak chest. She even thought that the lives of
many persons with a tendency to consumption might have been
prolonged, if they had learned to breathe, and sing, in the right
way—an opinion which is held by many medical authorities of
highest reputation, and the correctness of which is undoubtedly
proved by recorded facts; and she frequently expressed her con-
viction that the mode of living in England, and the care taken
of health, were very favourable indeed to the fuller development
of the physical frame, and, therefore, to the general vigour of
the vocal organs.

She also had a high opinion of the standard of musical
taste in England, and on one occasion, when speaking of the

different effect her singing produced on different audiences, she said she could distinctly feel that her listeners were not always swayed in the same manner by her power. "For instance," she said, "I always feel that music has a greater moral power over the English than over any other people, and this is why I would rather sing in *Oratorio* in this country than in any other."

So deeply penetrated was Madame Goldschmidt with love for her Art, and faith in its ennobling influence, that, to the end of her life, she took the keenest interest in promoting its instruction, upon the true and well-tried principles of the pure Italian School.

The following letter to the late Mr. H. C. Deacon* is one of the last she wrote upon the subject :—

"Wynd's Point, Colwall, Malvern, July 31st, 1885.

"DEAR MR. DEACON,

"It was very kind of you to let me know about the Examinations.† I am glad to hear that my *sheep* did not badly. If —— would put her mind into her work she might become a singer.

"I can but do my best; and, with my enormous experience and a life's study, I ought to be able to bring out singers.

"Singing is as much moral and mental as it is mechanical. It is the combination of those qualities which alone can form the master and pupil.

"I hope you and Mrs. Deacon are better, and that you will now have some rest.

"Yours sincerely,

"J. L. GOLDSCHMIDT."

With these remarks, we present the following *Cadenze*, *Solfeggi*, and *Abellimenti* to our readers, together with two of Mdlle. Lind's favourite Swedish Songs.

The *Solfeggi* (including the Study for practising the Shake, given at page 14) contain passages of great value to the aspiring vocalist.

The *Abellimenti* exemplify some of the most formidable difficulties in the practice of florid vocalisation.

The *Cadenze* are examples of a form of ornamentation which Madame Goldschmidt brought to a degree of perfection

---

* Madame Goldschmidt's colleague at the Royal College of Music, where she was then directing the training of the female vocal *Scholars*.

† At the Royal College of Music, above-mentioned.

previously unknown to the generation in which she lived, and
popularly supposed to have died out with the eighteenth
century. Madame Goldschmidt's *Cadenze* were original, in the
highest and best sense of the word—stamped with the rare
individuality of her artistic genius; in strict keeping with the
style of the music into which they were introduced ; and never
so introduced without a legitimate reason.* Most of these
were either written down by Mr. Goldschmidt, at her dictation,
or inserted, in her own handwriting, in the copies she herself
used, or in those of her pupils. Though some of the passages
they contain will be thought extremely difficult, it is hoped that
their careful study may be found useful, and do much towards
the cultivation, in the future, of this beautiful form of ornament,
the traditions of which are, it is to be feared, in danger of falling
into oblivion. The purity of the musical text is vouched for,
by the fact that, in every case, it is here given exactly as edited
by Mr. Otto Goldschmidt, in the " Musical Appendix " to the
work, entitled " JENNY LIND THE ARTIST.† A MEMOIR OF
MADAME JENNY LIND-GOLDSCHMIDT : HER EARLY ART-LIFE AND
DRAMATIC CAREER." By the Rev. Canon Scott Holland and
Mr. W. S. Rockstro. First published in 1891.

W. S. ROCKSTRO.

London, 1894.

---

* Madame Schumann, Herr Hauser, and others, give the like testimony to
Madame Goldschmidt's loyal rendering of Mozart's music. And it is evident
that the three *Cadenze* given in the present collection were supplied by her
because Mozart himself had indicated the place for their introduction.

† A few examples have been added for this publication.

MUSIC.

TABLE OF CONTENTS.

II

No 1.

Bellini's Opera *BEATRICE DI TENDA*· № 6 Cavatina(3 Cadenze.)

Cadenze b and c were by Madame Goldschmidt's permission included in the late Mr. H. C. Deacon's Article on "*Singing*" in Grove's Dictionary of Music. They are given here again together with Cadenza(a) in a form shewing the bars in which she introduced them at many Concerts.

Cadenza (b)
Oh - - -
accel.
rall.
mio ros - sor!
Allegro moderato.
Symphony
BEATRICE.
Ah! la
Più Allegro.
Coro
pe - na in lor piom - bò
Cadenza (c)
sempre p
rall.
a tempo
Ah! la pe - na in lor piom-bò
Stretto assai.
Symphony

IV _{*No. 2.*}

Bellini's *"I PURITANI"* Act II. Scena № 7. *Andante: Elvira,"Qui la voce."*

Madame Goldschmidt, more particularly in later years, when singing the *Andante* only—without the *Allegro* which follows— repeated the 17 bars at the end of this movement, substituting the *second* time instead of Bellini's bars 15 and 16 (in the voice part) the following two.

No. 3.

Donizetti's *"LUCIA DI LAMMERMOOR"* № 15. Cavatina (Paris. Published by Edmond Mayaud) *Larghetto* $\frac{9}{8}$ in G. *"Perchè non ho"* bar 33, Cadenza.✠)

✠) Introduced in Grove's Dictionary of Music and Musicians Vol. III. page 508, also in the Musical Union Record, 1849.

This Cadenza was sent to Ferdinand Hiller as a contribution to the well-known collection of Autographs which he left to the town of Cologne.

The inscription accompanying the Music is as follows *"Herrn Doctor Ferdinand von Hiller zur freundlichen Erinnerung von Jenny Lind-Goldschmidt.* London, November 1884."

Sehn - - - - - - - sucht.

N⁰ 5.

Mozart's *"DIE ZAUBERFLÖTE"* Act II. N⁰ 18. Aria. *Pamina.*

Ach   ich   fühl's,   es   ist   ver -
Ah!   lo   so,   più   non   m'a -

-schwunden, e - wig   Grab, den Weg in's Grab, den Weg_
-van-za   che lag - narmi   pe-nar, il mio pe-nar, il mi -

in's Grab.
- o pe - nar.

+) The Composer himself has placed this pause and indicated a Cadenza.

N° 6.

Mozart's Opera in two Acts "IL RE PASTORE" composed in 1775 (words by Metastasio) N° 10. Aria (with Violin obbligato.)

The following two *Cadenze* were composed in the autumn of 1854 by Madame Goldschmidt in collaboration with Herr Fr. Schubert (at the time First Concertmeister of the Royal Orchestra at Dresden.)

Madame Goldschmidt accompanied by Herr Schubert and subsequently by other Distinguished Violinists, sang the Aria with the addition of these *Cadenze*, at many Public Concerts, and also at Musical Festivals in Germany; they have not hitherto been published with authority.

+) Mozart has here indicated a Cadenza.

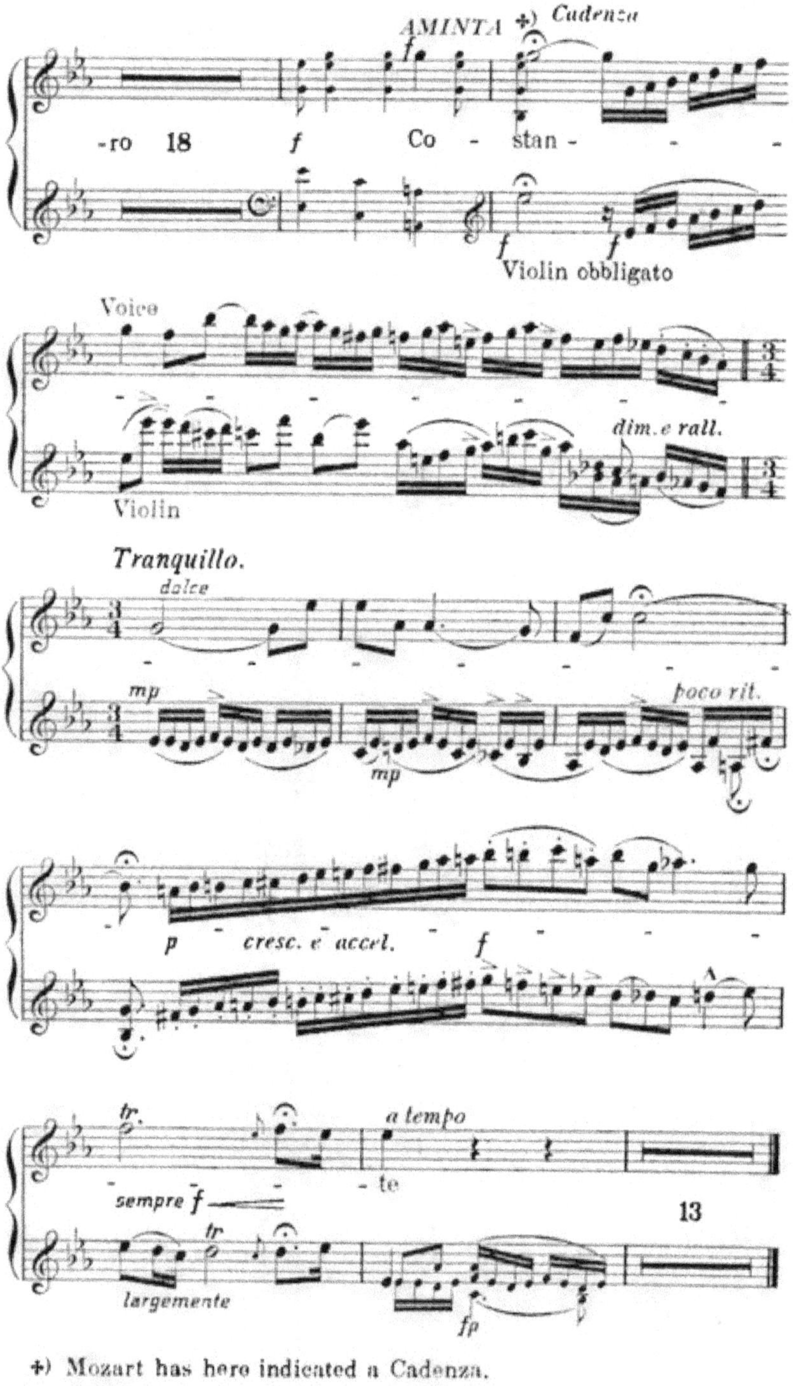

+) Mozart has here indicated a Cadenza.

N? 7.

The following Cadenza forms the ending of the *"RECUEIL DE MAZOURKAS de F. Chopin"* set to Italian words for (Soprano) Voice with Pianoforte obbligato(by Otto Goldschmidt) and sung by Madame Goldschmidt, from the year 1855, at her Concerts in Germany, Holland, and Great Britain.

The Mazourkas introduced are four, viz: Op. 50, N? 2. in A flat, Op. 30, N? 1. C minor, and N? 2. B minor, and lastly Op. 24, N? 3. of which Madame Goldschmidt sang the concluding strain, expanded on Chopin's own lines, as given on the next page in its entirety.

This "Recueil" has not been published.

Moscheles, having heard this piece, in November 1857, at the Gewandhaus at Leipzig, entered in his Diary the strain in bar 10, going up to the high C, differently, He wrote from recollection only; but in this form it has found a place not only in his Biography (Vol. II, London 1873) but also in Grove's Dictionary of Music Vol. II, page 141, and possibly elsewhere. Chopin's melody, however, had not been altered, and Madame Goldschmidt sang it as written by the Composer.

Moderato con anima. (Mazurka N? 3, Op. 24.)

Ri - man fe-del al tuo a - mor, al dolce fi-do a-mo - re

mai non pe-ri - rà ah!

Voice.

Pianof.

di - mi - nu - en - do

tranquillo

ah ma - i.

Pianof.

No 8.

Donizetti's "LA FIGLIA DEL REGGIMENTO" Finale of first Act.
4th bar from the end.

No 9.
FIVE SOLFEGGI.

I.
Allegretto (legato.)

+Translation "Come to me."

SOLFEGGI continued.

IV.

Ful -   -   -   -   -

-          -   -   -

-          -   -   -   -   - mi - ne.

V.

Son' -   -   -   -

-          -   -   -   -

-          -   -   -   - fe - li - ce.

Bellini's "*LA SONNAMBULA*" Aria "*Ah non credea*" from the Finale of the last Act as sung by Mademoiselle Lind on the Stage and subsequently at her Concerts by Madame Goldschmidt.

Andante cantabile.

AMINA.
espressivo

Ah! non cre-dea mi-rar- -ti Si pres-to e-stin-to, o fio- -re, Pas-sa-sti al par d'a-mo- -re Che un gior-no so-lo, cheun gior- -no sol du- -rò, che un gior-no

so - lo ah!_____ sol du - rò.

Pas - sa - sti al par d'a - mo -

- re, Che un

gior - no, che un gior - no sol_____ du - rò

Po - tria no - vel_____ vi -

- go - - re, Il pian - to, il pian - to mio re -

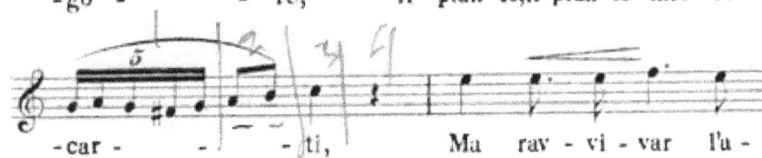

- car - - - ti, Ma rav - vi - var l'a -

- mo - - re il pian - - - - to

mi - o ah no, no non più ah non cre - de -

-a ah non cre-de - a, Pa-sa-sti al par, al par d'a-

-mo - - re che un gior - no sol _____ du -

-rò, che un gior-no sol du - rò, _____ che un

Lento.

gior - - - - no no

rall.

Cadenza tranquilla

accel. *tr*

sol _____ du -

-rò.

The embellishments of Cadenze in this piece were sung in moderate time, not quickly.

Nº 11.

The following Version of Rosina's Aria *"Una voce poco fà"* from Rossini's Opera *"IL BARBIERE DI SIVIGLIA,"* is that sung by Madame Goldschmidt.

The Air, having been originally written for a Contralto (in the key of E) must be transposed to a higher key, if sung by a Soprano; and in addition to this, various passages of low range have been traditionally altered, to suit the higher voice.

Madame Goldschmidt sang the Aria in the form given below (and in the key of F) at her Concerts, and taught it to the few select pupils who came under her care.

No indications of traditional changes of *Tempo* or marks of expression— save those introduced by Madame Goldschmidt— have been inserted here, as they are found in every good edition of the piece.

Andante.

12   ROSINA.

Symphony   U-na vo - ce po-co

fà   qui nel cor mi— ri - suo - nò   il mio

cor fe-ri-to è già   e— Lin - do-ro fù che il pia- -

-gò. Si, Lin - do - -ro— mio sa - rà, lo— giu-

-ra - i, la—— vin - ce - -rò, si, Lin-

-do - -ro mi - - -o sa-rà, lo giu- - -

-ra-i, la vin - - - - - - -ce-

-rò. Il tu-tor ri-cu-se-rò, Io l'in-gegno aguzze-

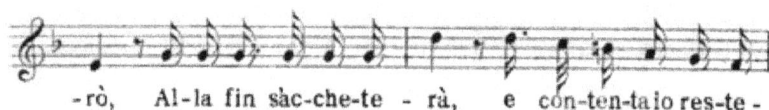

-rò, Al-la fin sàc-che-te - rà, e còn-ten-ta io res-te-

-rò, Si Lin - do - - ro__ mio__ sa -

-rà, lo_giu - ra-i, la__ vin - ce - rò, si Lin-

-do - - ro mi - - o sa-rà, lo_____ giu-

-ra-i la vin - - - - -

- - - - - - - -ce-rò.

Symphony Io so - - no do - ci - le,

son ri - spet - to - - sa, So - no ob - be -

-dien-te, dol - ce, a - mo - ro - - sa, Mi la-scio

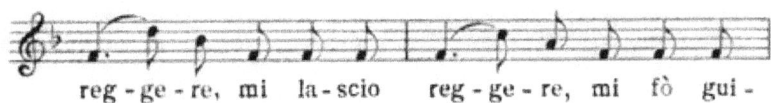

reg - ge - re, mi la-scio reg-ge-re, mi fò gui -

-dar, mi___ fò_____ gui - dar, Ma se mi

toc - -ca-no dov'e il mio de - - bo - le, come u - na

vi - - pe - - ra sa - rò, E cen - to

trap - -po-le pri-ma di ce - - de-re, fa-rò gio -

-car,___ fa - - rò___ gio - - car, e cen-to

trap - po - le pri - ma di ce - de - re, fa - rò glo -

-car_ fa - -rò gio - -ca-re, e_ cen-to_

sonore

trap-po-le pri-ma_ di ce - de-re, e cen-to

pp

trap-po- -le fa - -rò, fa - -rò gio-

Viol.   Viol.

-car.   Io so-no do-ci-le,

so-no obbediente mi lascio regge-re mi fò giu-

rall.   *a tempo*

-da - - - - - re Ma se mi

toc - ca - no dov' il mio de - bo - le come u-na

vi - -pe - ra_____ sa - rò,_ e cen-to

trap-po - le, pri-ma di ce - de - re, fa-rò gio-

-ca - - - - re, e cen - to

con abandon

trap - po - le, pri - ma di ce - de - re fa - rò gio -

-car, fa - rò gio - - ca - re, e cen - to

trap - po - le pri - - ma di ce-de-re, e cen-to

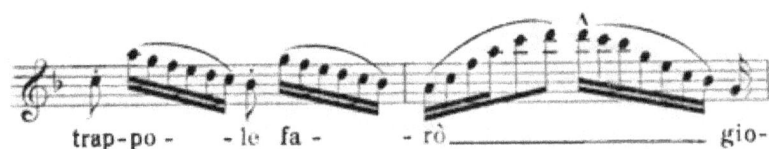

trap - po - le fa - - rò gio-

-car, e cen - to trap - po - le fa - rò gio -

-car, e cen - to trap - po - le fa - rò gio -

-car, fa - rò gio - car, fa - rò gio -

-car, fa - - rò gio - car. Symphony

This is the Version transcribed from the (late) Courtsinger L.A. Berg's own Mss. Musicbook, now in the possession of his son, whose kind permission it is inserted here.

HERDEGOSSEN. [A]

Fjer-ran i skog

Långt från dig skiljd. Klar för min själ Strå-lar din bild

Hor - net min kla-gan till dig nu

för Ger-na! Ger-na för dig jag dör.

This is the Version sung in Public by Madame Goldschmidt both in
Europe and in America, and in Private up to a late period of her life.

HERDEGOSSEN. [B]

THE HERDSMAN'S SONG.

Composed by

I. A. BERG.

Andante lento. dolce

Fjer-ran i skog   Långt från dig
Far in the woods   *Part-ed from*

skiljd   Klar för min själ   Strå - lar din
thee,   *Thine i-mage fair*   *Still dwells with*

bild   Hor - net min kla - gan
me   *So let the horn breathe my*

till - dig för Ger - na, ack! ger-na för dig jag
se - cret to thee: Death for my love hath no ter-ror for

dör. Hor - net min kla - gan
me. So let the horn breathe my

till - dig för Ger - na, ack! gerna, ger - na
se - cret to thee: Death for my love hath no

för dig dör.
ter - ror for me.

NORWEGIAN ECHO SONG.

The following Norwegian Popular melody has been referred to more than once in the preceding Volumes, and in one instance by M^{dlle} Lind herself, in a letter dated Boston November 8. 1850. (See Book IX, Ch. V.) in which she calls it the Norwegian Fjäll (Fell) Song.

The version given here is as nearly what she sang, as a wild original piece of National Music, subject to many variations in detail at the humour of the Singer, (who invariably accompanied it herself on the Pianoforte) can be put on paper.

The unaccompanied *Coda* at the close, introducing an Echo, was added by the Songstress, and has, it is thought, not hitherto been printed.

The Norwegian words only are here inserted, but a translation of the simple sense of the words will be found at the end of the Song.

Allegretto.

sonore e in Tempo moderato

Kom kjyra, kom kjyra mi! Kom kjyra,   Hoah, hoah,

hoah, hoah,   trr   ho, ho!   Kom ku, kom kalv, kom kjy-ra, Kom al-le di und-li-a dy-ra! Å sme-en kom from me

ham-mer å tang, Sat-te de merkje på stu-te-horn de

parlando

più sonore

vål-te den Skalkuli bergaman! Hoah, hoah, hoah! Kom al-

-le kjy-ra mi, å stakkar!

Moderato.
dolce

So-len går bak å sen nen Skyggjen bli så langje,

XXVI

nåt-te kjem snart at - te -ve, teck-je meg___ i fan - ge.

Vivo.
Krytrein u -ti kvien står___ eg te sae-ter-stu-li går!

con forza
Kritrein u -ti kvi-en står- -eg te sae - ter-stu-li går!

Molto Allegro.

Tempo I.
Kom kjy -ra, kom kjyra mi kom kjy-ra!___

Hoah, hoah, hoah, hoah   trr____   ho, ho. Ah

Moderato.   *dim.*

accel.   *Moderato.*   *Lento*
ad lib. Ah____ Ah____ Ah____

+) At this point Madame Goldschmidt turned from the Pianoforte towards the audience, facing it, and singing straight towards the length of the Room (having in view the production of the Echo) until the final notes, when she *slowly* turned back towards the Pianoforte, and struck the Chord of D to the same note in the voice part.

(Translation.)

Come hither, come hither, come hither!
 Hoah, hoah, hoah!
Come cow, come calf and weanling brood
Come all my cattle dear!
And the smith come forth
With hammer and tongs
To put the brand on the animal
For so will have it the Sheriff done.
 Hoah, hoah, hoah!
Come all ye my poor dear!

The sun is setting behind the hills
And shadows are lengthning;
The night will soon close in
And hold us in its lap.
 The pot is on the fire
 And to the Alp I wend my way.

October, 1894.   *Finis.*

www.ingramcontent.com/pod-product-compliance
Lightning Source LLC
Chambersburg PA
CBHW021554270326
41931CB00009B/1206